THE

PEACE

BOOK

Teachings from the
Greatest Minds
of All Time

CIDER MILL
PRESS

BOOK
PUBLISHERS
KENNEBUNKPORT, MAINE

THE PEACE BOOK

13-Digit ISBN: 978-1-64643-324-7
10-Digit ISBN: 1-64643-324-6

This book may be ordered by mail from the publisher. Please include $5.99 for postage and handling. Please support your local bookseller first!

Books published by Cider Mill Press Book Publishers are available at special discounts for bulk purchases in the United States by corporations, institutions, and other organizations. For more information, please contact the publisher.

Cider Mill Press Book Publishers
"Where good books are ready for press"
PO Box 454
12 Spring Street
Kennebunkport, Maine 04046

Visit us online!
cidermillpress.com

Typography: Mr Eaves Sans, Mrs Eaves Serif, Type Embellishments One

All images used under official license from Shutterstock.com.

Printed in Malaysia

1 2 3 4 5 6 7 8 9 0

First Edition

CONTENTS

INTRODUCTION

Many of us, when asked, would claim that one of our greatest wishes is world peace. Most of us also say that we would like to find inner peace. And practically everyone is clear about wanting peace in their relationships with their friends and loved ones. But how many of us are actually actively thinking about and pursuing peace?

Between the stresses of daily life, the struggle to maintain friendships and romantic relationships, and the occasionally crushing weight of the world's problems, it's no wonder that we have trouble tackling all the things we are burdened with. Sometimes it's all we can do just to keep our heads above water.

Our hope is that this book will inspire you to find new ways to see and solve life's problems. With insights from great minds pulled from across the centuries, you are sure to find something that speaks to you. Read a new page every day to keep peace present in your life, or flip to a section that deals with the kind of peace you need right now. Whether you're trying to find peace of mind or a peaceful resolution, or you just want to be reminded that hatred is not the ruler of this world, there is something here for you.

In this book, there are quotes, poems, speeches, excerpts from plays and literature, and even playlists, all specifically curated to help you find whatever peace it is you are seeking. Let them inspire you to create and spread peace wherever you go, be it in yourself, to your friends, or beyond; you have the power to help bring peace to the world through the way you think and act. *The Peace Book* is just the beginning.

INNER PEACE

"DO NOT LET THE BEHAVIOR OF OTHERS DESTROY YOUR INNER PEACE."

— the 14th Dalai Lama

GOOD-NIGHT

PAUL LAURENCE DUNBAR

The lark is silent in his nest,
　The breeze is sighing in its flight,
Sleep, Love, and peaceful be thy rest.
　Good-night, my love, good-night, good-night.

Sweet dreams attend thee in thy sleep,
　To soothe thy rest till morning's light,
And angels round thee vigil keep.
　Good-night, my love, good-night, good-night.

Sleep well, my love, on night's dark breast,
　And ease thy soul with slumber bright;
Be joy but thine and I am blest.
　Good-night, my love, good-night, good-night.

REPENTANCE

AMEEN RIHANI

When tears wash tears and soul upon soul leaps,
  When clasped in arms of anguish and of pain,
When love beneath the feet of passion creeps,
  Ah me, what do we gain?

When we our rosy bower to demons lease,
  When Life's most tender strains by shrieks are slain,
When strife invades our quietude and peace,
  Ah me, what do we gain?

When we allow the herbs of hate to sprout,
  When weeds of jealousy the lily stain,
When pearls of faith are crushed by stones of doubt,
  Ah me, what do we gain?

When night creeps on us in the light of day,
  When we nepenthes of good cheer disdain,
When on the throne of courage sits dismay,
  Ah me, what do we gain?

When sweetness, goodness, kindness all have died,
  When naught but broken, bleeding hearts remain,
When rough-shod o'er our better self we ride,
  Ah me, what do we gain?

NATURE'S PEACE WILL FLOW INTO YOU AS SUNSHINE FLOWS INTO TREES. THE WINDS WILL BLOW THEIR OWN FRESHNESS INTO YOU, AND THE STORMS THEIR ENERGY, WHILE CARES WILL DROP OFF LIKE AUTUMN LEAVES. AS AGE COMES ON, ONE SOURCE OF ENJOYMENT AFTER ANOTHER IS CLOSED, BUT NATURE'S SOURCES NEVER FAIL. LIKE A GENEROUS HOST, SHE OFFERS HERE BRIMMING CUPS IN ENDLESS VARIETY, SERVED IN A GRAND HALL, THE SKY ITS CEILING, THE MOUNTAINS ITS WALLS, DECORATED WITH GLORIOUS PAINTINGS AND ENLIVENED WITH BANDS OF MUSIC EVER PLAYING.

—John Muir, *Our National Parks*

"PEACE COMES FROM WITHIN. DO NOT SEEK IT WITHOUT."

—Gautama Buddha

EXCERPT FROM
NATURE
RALPH WALDO EMERSON

To go into solitude, a man needs to retire as much from his chamber as from society. I am not solitary whilst I read and write, though nobody is with me. But if a man would be alone, let him look at the stars. The rays that come from those heavenly worlds, will separate between him and what he touches. One might think the atmosphere was made transparent with this design, to give man, in the heavenly bodies, the perpetual presence of the sublime. Seen in the streets of cities, how great they are! If the stars should appear one night in a thousand years, how would men believe and adore; and preserve for many generations the remembrance of the city of God which had been shown! But every night come out these envoys of beauty, and light the universe with their admonishing smile.

The stars awaken a certain reverence, because though always present, they are inaccessible; but all natural objects make a kindred impression, when the mind is open to their influence. Nature never wears a mean appearance. Neither does the wisest man extort her secret, and lose his curiosity by finding out all her perfection. Nature never became a toy to a wise spirit. The flowers, the animals, the mountains, reflected the wisdom of his best hour, as much as they had delighted the simplicity of his childhood.

When we speak of nature in this manner, we have a distinct but most poetical sense in the mind. We mean the integrity of impression made by manifold natural objects. It is this which distinguishes the stick of timber of the wood-cutter, from the tree of the poet. The charming landscape which I saw this morning, is indubitably made up of some twenty or thirty farms. Miller owns this field, Locke that, and Manning the woodland beyond. But none of them owns the landscape. There is a property in the horizon which no man has but he whose eye can integrate all the parts, that is, the poet. This is the best part of these men's farms, yet to this their warranty-deeds give no title.

To speak truly, few adult persons can see nature. Most persons do not see the sun. At least they have a very superficial seeing. The sun illuminates only the eye of the man, but shines into the eye and the heart of the child. The lover of nature is he whose inward and outward senses are still truly adjusted to each other; who has retained the spirit of infancy even into the era of manhood. His intercourse with heaven and earth, becomes part of his daily food. In the presence of nature, a wild delight runs through the man, in spite of real sorrows. Nature says,—he is my creature, and maugre all his impertinent griefs, he shall be glad with me. Not the sun or the summer alone, but every hour and season yields its tribute of delight; for every hour and change corresponds to and authorizes a different state of the mind, from breathless noon to grimmest midnight. Nature is a setting that fits equally well a comic or a mourning piece. In good health, the air is a cordial of incredible virtue. Crossing a bare common, in snow puddles, at twilight, under a clouded sky, without having in my thoughts any occurrence of special good fortune, I have enjoyed a perfect exhilaration. I am glad to the brink of fear. In the woods too, a man casts off his years, as the snake his slough, and at what period soever of life, is always a child. In the woods, is perpetual youth. Within these plantations of God, a decorum and sanctity reign, a perennial festival is dressed, and the guest sees not how he should tire of them in a thousand years. In the woods, we return to reason and faith. There I feel that nothing can befall me in life,—no disgrace, no calamity, (leaving me my eyes,) which nature cannot repair. Standing on the bare ground,—my head bathed by the blithe air, and uplifted into infinite space,—all mean egotism vanishes. I become a transparent eye-ball; I am nothing; I see all; the currents of the Universal Being circulate through me; I am part or particle of God. The name of the nearest friend sounds then foreign and accidental: to be brothers, to be acquaintances,—master or servant, is then a trifle and a disturbance.

I am the lover of uncontained and immortal beauty. In the wilderness, I find something more dear and connate than in streets or villages. In the tranquil landscape, and especially in the distant line of the horizon, man beholds somewhat as beautiful as his own nature.

The greatest delight which the fields and woods minister, is the suggestion of an occult relation between man and the vegetable. I am not alone and unacknowledged. They nod to me, and I to them. The waving of the boughs in the storm, is new to me and old. It takes me by surprise, and yet is not unknown. Its effect is like that of a higher thought or a better emotion coming over me, when I deemed I was thinking justly or doing right.

Yet it is certain that the power to produce this delight, does not reside in nature, but in man, or in a harmony of both. It is necessary to use these pleasures with great temperance. For, nature is not always tricked in holiday attire, but the same scene which yesterday breathed perfume and glittered as for the frolic of the nymphs, is overspread with melancholy today. Nature always wears the colors of the spirit. To a man laboring under calamity, the heat of his own fire hath sadness in it. Then, there is a kind of contempt of the landscape felt by him who has just lost by death a dear friend. The sky is less grand as it shuts down over less worth in the population.

IF YOU BECOME
RESTLESS, SPEED
UP. IF YOU BECOME
WINDED, SLOW
DOWN. YOU CLIMB
THE MOUNTAIN IN
AN EQUILIBRIUM
BETWEEN
RESTLESSNESS AND
EXHAUSTION.

—Robert M. Pirsig,
Zen and the Art of Motorcycle Maintenance

"IF YOU ARE DEPRESSED, YOU ARE LIVING IN THE PAST. IF YOU ARE ANXIOUS, YOU ARE LIVING IN THE FUTURE. IF YOU ARE AT PEACE, YOU ARE LIVING IN THE PRESENT."

—Lao Tzu

EXCERPT FROM
ASPHODEL, THAT GREENY FLOWER
WILLIAM CARLOS WILLIAMS

My heart rouses
            thinking to bring you news
                        of something
that concerns you
            and concerns many men. Look at
                        what passes for the new.
You will not find it there but in
            despised poems.
                        It is difficult
to get the news from poems
            yet men die miserably every day
                        for lack
of what is found there.
            Hear me out
                        for I too am concerned
and every man
            who wants to die at peace in his bed
                        besides.

"TRUE HAPPINESS IS TO ENJOY THE PRESENT, WITHOUT ANXIOUS DEPENDENCE UPON THE FUTURE."

—Seneca

IT IS ONLY WITH
TOTAL HUMILITY,
AND IN ABSOLUTE
STILLNESS OF
MIND THAT WE
CAN KNOW WHAT
INDEED WE ARE.

—Wei Wu Wei, *The Tenth Man: The Great Joke*

MY SPIRIT WILL
SLEEP IN PEACE;
OR IF IT THINKS, IT
WILL NOT SURELY
THINK THUS.
FAREWELL.

—Mary Shelley, *Frankenstein*

SONGS ABOUT PEACE OF MIND

Don't Worry, Be Happy: **Bobby McFerrin**

Perfect Day: **Lou Reed**

Happy: **Pharell Williams**

Best Day of My Life: **American Authors**

Walking on Sunshine: **Katrina and the Waves**

Three Little Birds: **Bob Marley & the Wailers**

Put Your Records On: **Corinne Bailey Rae**

I Can See Clearly Now: **Johnny Nash**

The Remedy (I Won't Worry): **Jason Mraz**

Holocene: **Bon Iver**

Good Vibrations: **The Beach Boys**

It's a Beautiful Day: **Michael Bublé**

Good Life: **OneRepublic**

Lovely Day: **Bill Withers**

PEACE

SARA TEASDALE

Peace flows into me
As the tide to the pool by the shore;
It is mine forevermore,
It ebbs not back like the sea.

I am the pool of blue
That worships the vivid sky;
My hopes were heaven-high,
They are all fulfilled in you.

I am the pool of gold
When sunset burns and dies,—
You are my deepening skies,
Give me your stars to hold.

KNOW YOUR OWN
HAPPINESS. YOU
WANT NOTHING
BUT PATIENCE—OR
GIVE IT A MORE
FASCINATING
NAME, CALL
IT HOPE.

—Jane Austen, *Sense and Sensibility*

IT IS NOT
LIFE THAT'S
COMPLICATED,
IT'S THE
STRUGGLE TO
GUIDE AND
CONTROL LIFE.

—F. Scott Fitzgerald, *This Side of Paradise*

HENRY DAVID THOREAU
REFLECTS ON NATURE, 1854

We must learn to reawaken and keep ourselves awake, not by mechanical aids, but by an infinite expectation of the dawn, which does not forsake us in our soundest sleep. I know of no more encouraging fact than the unquestionable ability of man to elevate his life by a conscious endeavor. It is something to be able to paint a particular picture, or to carve a statue, and so to make a few objects beautiful; but it is far more glorious to carve and paint the very atmosphere and medium through which we look, which morally we can do. To affect the quality of the day, that is the highest of arts. Every man is tasked to make his life, even in its details, worthy of the contemplation of his most elevated and critical hour. If we refused, or rather used up, such paltry information as we get, the oracles would distinctly inform us how this might be done.

I went to the woods because I wished to live deliberately, to front only the essential facts of life, and see if I could not learn what it had to teach, and not, when I came to die, discover that I had not lived. I did not wish to live what was not life, living is so dear; nor did I wish to practise resignation, unless it was quite necessary. I wanted to live deep and suck out all the marrow of life, to live so sturdily and Spartan-like as to put to rout all that was not life, to cut a broad swath and shave close, to drive life into a corner, and reduce it to its lowest terms, and, if it proved to be mean, why then to get the whole and genuine meanness of it, and publish its meanness to the world; or if it were sublime, to know it by experience, and be able to give a true account of it in my next excursion. For most men, it appears to me, are in a strange uncertainty about it, whether it is of the devil or of God, and have *somewhat hastily* concluded that it is the chief end of man here to "glorify God and enjoy him forever."

Still we live meanly, like ants; though the fable tells us that we were long ago changed into men; like pygmies we fight with cranes; it is error upon error, and clout upon clout, and our best virtue has for its occasion a superfluous and evitable wretchedness. Our life is frittered away by detail. An honest man has hardly need to count more than his ten fingers, or in extreme cases he may add his ten toes, and lump the rest. Simplicity, simplicity, simplicity! I say, let your affairs be as two or three, and not a hundred or a thousand; instead of a million count half a dozen, and keep your accounts on your thumb-nail. In the midst of this chopping sea of civilized life, such are the clouds and storms and quick-sands and thousand-and-one items to be allowed for, that a man has to live, if he would not founder and go to the bottom and not make his port at all, by dead reck-oning, and he must be a great calculator indeed who succeeds. Simplify, simplify. Instead of three meals a day, if it be necessary eat but one; instead of a hundred dishes, five; and reduce other things in proportion. Our life is like a German Confederacy, made up of petty states, with its boundary forever fluctuating, so that even a German cannot tell you how it is bounded at any moment. The nation itself, with all its so-called internal improvements, which, by the way are all external and superficial, is just such an unwieldy and overgrown establishment, cluttered with furniture and tripped up by its own traps, ruined by luxury and heedless expense, by want of calculation and a worthy aim, as the million households in the land; and the only cure for it, as for them, is in a rigid economy, a stern and more than Spartan simplicity of life and elevation of purpose. It lives too fast. Men think that it is essential that the *Nation* have commerce, and export ice, and talk through a telegraph, and ride thirty miles an hour, without a doubt, whether *they* do or not; but whether we should live like baboons or like men, is a little uncertain. If we do not get out sleepers, and forge rails, and devote days and nights to the work, but go to tinkering upon our *lives* to improve *them*, who will build railroads? And if railroads are not built, how shall we get to heaven in season? But if we stay at home and mind our business, who will want railroads? We do not ride on the railroad; it rides upon us. Did you ever think what those sleepers are that underlie the railroad? Each one is a man, an Irishman, or a Yankee man. The rails are laid on them, and they are covered with sand, and the cars run smoothly over them. They are sound sleepers, I assure you. And every few years a new lot is laid down and run over; so that, if some have the pleasure of riding on a rail, others have the misfortune to be ridden upon. And when they run over a man that is walking in his sleep, a supernumerary sleeper in the wrong position, and wake him up, they suddenly stop the cars, and make a hue and cry about it, as if this were an exception. I am glad to know that it takes a gang of men for every five miles to keep the sleepers down and level in their beds as it is, for this is a sign that they may sometime get up again.

"WHEN WE START
TO FEEL ANXIOUS
OR DEPRESSED,
INSTEAD OF ASKING,
'WHAT DO I NEED TO
GET TO BE HAPPY?'
THE QUESTION
BECOMES, 'WHAT
AM I DOING TO
DISTURB THE INNER
PEACE THAT I
ALREADY HAVE?'"

—D. T. Suzuki

MANY PEOPLE THINK EXCITEMENT IS HAPPINESS....BUT WHEN YOU ARE EXCITED YOU ARE NOT PEACEFUL. TRUE HAPPINESS IS BASED ON PEACE.

—Thich Nhat Hanh, *The Art of Power*

IT WAS NOT FATE

WILLIAM MOORE

It was not fate which overtook me,
Rather a wayward, wilful wind
That blew hot for awhile
And then, as the even shadows came, blew cold.
What pity it is that a man grown old in life's dreaming
Should stop, e'en for a moment, to look into a woman's eyes.
And I forgot!
Forgot that one's heart must be steeled against the east wind.
Life and death alike come out of the East:
Life as tender as young grass,
Death as dreadful as the sight of clotted blood.
I shall go back into the darkness,
Not to dream but to seek the light again.
I shall go by paths, mayhap,
On roads that wind around the foothills
Where the plains are bare and wild
And the passers-by come few and far between.
I want the night to be long, the moon blind.
The hills thick with moving memories,
And my heart beating a breathless requiem
For all the dead days I have lived.
When the Dawn comes—Dawn, deathless, dreaming—
I shall will that my soul must be cleansed of hate,
I shall pray for strength to hold children close to my heart,
I shall desire to build houses where the poor will know
    shelter, comfort, beauty.
And then may I look into a woman's eyes
And find holiness, love and the peace which passeth understanding.

THOUGHTS

MYRA VIOLA WILDS

What kind of thoughts now, do you carry
  In your travels day by day
Are they bright and lofty visions,
  Or neglected, gone astray?

Matters not how great in fancy,
  Or what deeds of skill you've wrought;
Man, though high may be his station,
  Is no better than his thoughts.

Catch your thoughts and hold them tightly,
  Let each one an honor be;
Purge them, scourge them, burnish brightly,
  Then in love set each one free.

"SERENITY IS NOT FREEDOM FROM THE STORM, BUT PEACE AMID THE STORM."

—Anonymous

"NEVER BE IN A HURRY; DO EVERYTHING QUIETLY AND IN A CALM SPIRIT. DO NOT LOSE YOUR PEACE FOR ANYTHING WHATSOEVER, EVEN IF YOUR WHOLE WORLD SEEMS UPSET."

—Saint Francis de Sales

"WE CAN NEVER OBTAIN PEACE IN THE OUTER WORLD UNTIL WE MAKE PEACE WITH OURSELVES."

— the 14th Dalai Lama

WHEN THE FROST IS ON THE PUNKIN

JAMES WHITCOMB RILEY

When the frost is on the punkin and the fodder's in the shock,

And you hear the kyouck and gobble of the struttin' turkey-cock,

And the clackin' of the guineys, and the cluckin' of the hens,

And the rooster's hallylooer as he tiptoes on the fence;

O, it's then's the times a feller is a-feelin' at his best,

With the risin' sun to greet him from a night of peaceful rest,

As he leaves the house, bareheaded, and goes out to feed the
  stock,

When the frost is on the punkin and the fodder's in the shock.

They's something kindo' harty-like about the atmusfere

When the heat of summer's over and the coolin' fall is here—

Of course we miss the flowers, and the blossums on the trees,

And the mumble of the hummin'-birds and buzzin' of the bees;

But the air's so appetizin'; and the landscape through the haze

Of a crisp and sunny morning of the airly autumn days

Is a pictur' that no painter has the colorin' to mock—

When the frost is on the punkin and the fodder's in the shock.

The husky, rusty russel of the tossels of the corn,

And the raspin' of the tangled leaves, as golden as the morn;

The stubble in the furries—kindo' lonesome-like, but still

A-preachin' sermuns to us of the barns they growed to fill;

The strawstack in the medder, and the reaper in the shed;

The hosses in theyr stalls below—the clover over-head!—

O, it sets my hart a-clickin' like the tickin' of a clock,

When the frost is on the punkin and the fodder's in the shock!

Then your apples all is gethered, and the ones a feller keeps

Is poured around the celler-floor in red and yeller heaps;

And your cider-makin' 's over, and your wimmern-folks is through

With their mince and apple-butter, and theyr souse and saussage, too!...

I don't know how to tell it—but ef sich a thing could be

As the Angels wantin' boardin', and they'd call around on *me*—

I'd want to 'commodate 'em—all the whole-indurin' flock—

When the frost is on the punkin and the fodder's in the shock!

IN PEACE THERE'S
NOTHING SO
BECOMES A MAN
AS MODEST
STILLNESS AND
HUMILITY.

—William Shakespeare, *Henry V*

CHAMBER MUSIC

JAMES JOYCE

Sleep now, O sleep now,
　O you unquiet heart!
A voice crying "Sleep now"
　Is heard in my heart.

The voice of the winter
　Is heard at the door.
O sleep, for the winter
　Is crying "Sleep no more."

My kiss will give peace now
　And quiet to your heart—
Sleep on in peace now,
　O you unquiet heart!

"FOLLOW THE STREAM,
HAVE FAITH IN ITS
COURSE. IT WILL GO
ON ITS OWN WAY,
MEANDERING HERE,
TRICKLING THERE.
IT WILL FIND THE
GROOVES, THE CRACKS,
THE CREVICES. JUST
FOLLOW IT. NEVER LET
IT OUT OF YOUR SIGHT.
IT WILL TAKE YOU."

—Sheng-yen

NOBODY CAN
BRING YOU PEACE
BUT YOURSELF.
NOTHING CAN
BRING YOU PEACE
BUT THE TRIUMPH
OF PRINCIPLES.

—Ralph Waldo Emerson, *Self-Reliance*

FOR THE BIRD SINGING BEFORE DAWN

KIM STAFFORD

Some people presume to be hopeful
when there is no evidence for hope,
to be happy when there is no cause.
Let me say now, I'm with them.

In deep darkness on a cold twig
in a dangerous world, one first
little fluff lets out a peep, a warble,
a song—and in a little while, behold:

the first glimmer comes, then a glow
filters through the misty trees,
then the bold sun rises, then
everyone starts bustling about.

And that first crazy optimist, can we
forgive her for thinking, dawn by dawn,
"Hey, I made that happen!
And oh, life is so fine."

"THE MIND CAN GO IN A THOUSAND DIRECTIONS, BUT ON THIS BEAUTIFUL PATH, I WALK IN PEACE. WITH EACH STEP, THE WIND BLOWS. WITH EACH STEP, A FLOWER BLOOMS."

—Thich Nhat Hanh

O SUN OF REAL PEACE

WALT WHITMAN

O sun of real peace! O hastening light!

O free and extatic! O what I here, preparing, warble for!

O the sun of the world will ascend, dazzling, and take his height—and you too, O my Ideal, will surely ascend!

O so amazing and broad—up there resplendent, darting and burning!

O vision prophetic, stagger'd with weight of light! with pouring glories!

O lips of my soul, already becoming powerless!

O ample and grand Presidentiads! Now the war, the war is over!

New history! new heroes! I project you!

Visions of poets! only you really last! sweep on! sweep on!

O heights too swift and dizzy yet!

O purged and luminous! you threaten me more than I can stand!

(I must not venture—the ground under my feet menaces me—

it will not support me: O future too immense,)—

O present, I return, while yet I may, to you.

DO YOU HAVE THE PATIENCE TO WAIT UNTIL YOUR MUD SETTLES AND THE WATER IS CLEAR?

—Lao Tzu, *Tao Te Ching*

FOR HOW CAN
ONE KNOW
COLOR IN
PERPETUAL
GREEN, AND
WHAT GOOD
IS WARMTH
WITHOUT COLD
TO GIVE IT
SWEETNESS?

—John Steinbeck,
Travels with Charley: In Search of America

PEACE
BETWEEN
FRIENDS

AHEAD AND AROUND

LAURA RIDING JACKSON

Ahead and Around
Met, quarreled, quilled the bird of peace,
Untidied a pleasant plane.
Ahead accused Around of complete deceit,
Around accused Ahead of being discontented.
Neither listened to each.
Either lined on,
Making round straight and straight round,
Permitting nothing in-between,
Licked space clean,
Fattened unhappily and flew
Along the geometrical faith of two-and-two,
Hated apart; and far and far
Each wanderer
Hoped toward a spiritually reconnoitered heaven.

"For," cried sinuous Around,
"More and less than I, am I,
Nature of all things, all things the nature of me."
Ahead echoed the cry.
Sped toward its own eternity

Of the sweet end before the bitter beyond, beyond.
And both were brave and both were strong,
And the ways of both were like and long,
And adventured freely in fettered song:
One that circled as it sang,
One that longitudinally rang.

The spite prospered. The spite stopped.
Both earned the same end differently,
Prided along two different paths,
Reached the same humility
Of an old-trodden start.
Birth is the beginning where all part.
Death is the beginning where they meet.

"A PEACE IS OF THE NATURE OF A CONQUEST; FOR THEN BOTH PARTIES NOBLY ARE SUBDUED, AND NEITHER PARTY LOSER."

—William Shakespeare

"ONE OF THE MOST BEAUTIFUL QUALITIES OF TRUE FRIENDSHIP IS TO UNDERSTAND AND TO BE UNDERSTOOD."

—Seneca

ON FRIENDSHIP

KAHLIL GIBRAN

And a youth said, Speak to us of Friendship.

And he answered, saying:

Your friend is your needs answered.

He is your field which you sow with love and reap with thanksgiving.

And he is your board and your fireside.

For you come to him with your hunger, and you seek him for peace.

When your friend speaks his mind you fear not the "nay" in your own mind, nor do you withhold the "ay."

And when he is silent your heart ceases not to listen to his heart;

For without words, in friendship, all thoughts, all desires, all expectations are born and shared, with joy that is unacclaimed.

When you part from your friend, you grieve not;

For that which you love most in him may be clearer in his absence, as the mountain to the climber is clearer from the plain.

And let there be no purpose in friendship save the deepening of the spirit.

For love that seeks aught but the disclosure of its own mystery is not love but a net cast forth: and only the unprofitable is caught.

And let your best be for your friend.

If he must know the ebb of your tide, let him know its flood also.

For what is your friend that you should seek him with hours to kill?

Seek him always with hours to live.

For it is his to fill your need but not your emptiness.

And in the sweetness of friendship let there be laughter, and sharing of pleasures.

For in the dew of little things the heart finds its morning and is refreshed.

LOVE AND FRIENDSHIP

EMILY BRONTË

Love is like the wild rose-briar,
Friendship like the holly-tree—
The holly is dark when the rose-briar blooms
But which will bloom most constantly?

The wild rose-briar is sweet in spring,
Its summer blossoms scent the air;
Yet wait till winter comes again
And who will call the wild-briar fair?

Then scorn the silly rose-wreath now
And deck thee with the holly's sheen,
That when December blights thy brow
He still may leave thy garland green.

"SPREAD LOVE EVERYWHERE YOU GO....LET NO ONE EVER COME TO YOU WITHOUT LEAVING HAPPIER."

—Mother Teresa

I HAVE PERCEIV'D
THAT TO BE WITH
THOSE I LIKE IS
ENOUGH.

—Walt Whitman, *I Sing the Body Electric*

EXCERPT FROM
FRIENDSHIP
RALPH WALDO EMERSON

I do not wish to treat friendships daintily, but with roughest courage. When they are real, they are not glass threads or frostwork, but the solidest thing we know. For now, after so many ages of experience, what do we know of nature, or of ourselves? Not one step has man taken toward the solution of the problem of his destiny. In one condemnation of folly stand the whole universe of men. But the sweet sincerity of joy and peace, which I draw from this alliance with my brother's soul, is the nut itself, whereof all nature and all thought is but the husk and shell. Happy is the house that shelters a friend! It might well be built, like a festal bower or arch, to entertain him a single day. Happier, if he know the solemnity of that relation, and honor its law! He who offers himself a candidate for that covenant comes up, like an Olympian, to the great games, where the first-born of the world are the competitors. He proposes himself for contests where Time, Want, Danger, are in the lists, and he alone is victor who has truth enough in his constitution to preserve the delicacy of his beauty from the wear and tear of all these. The gifts of fortune may be present or absent, but all the speed in that contest depends on intrinsic nobleness, and the contempt of trifles. There are two elements that go to the composition of friendship, each so sovereign that I can detect no superiority in either, no reason why either should be first named. One is Truth. A friend is a person with whom I may be sincere. Before him I may think aloud. I am arrived at last in the presence of a man so real and equal, that I may drop even those undermost garments of dissimulation, courtesy, and second thought, which men never put off, and may deal with him with the simplicity and wholeness with which one chemical atom meets another. Sincerity is the luxury allowed, like diadems and authority, only to the highest rank, that being permitted to speak truth, as having none above it to court or conform unto. Every man alone is sincere. At the entrance of a second person, hypocrisy begins. We parry and fend the approach of our fellow-man by compliments, by gossip, by amusements, by affairs. We cover up our thought from him under a hundred folds. I knew a man, who, under a certain religious frenzy, cast off this drapery, and, omitting all compliment and commonplace, spoke to the conscience of every person he encountered, and that with great insight and beauty. At first he was resisted, and all men agreed he was mad. But persisting, as indeed he could not help doing, for some time in this course, he attained to the advantage of bringing every man of his acquaintance into true relations with him. No man would think of speaking falsely with him, or of putting him off with any chat of markets or reading-rooms.

But every man was constrained by so much sincerity to the like plaindealing, and what love of nature, what poetry, what symbol of truth he had, he did certainly show him. But to most of us society shows not its face and eye, but its side and its back. To stand in true relations with men in a false age is worth a fit of insanity, is it not? We can seldom go erect. Almost every man we meet requires some civility,—requires to be humored; he has some fame, some talent, some whim of religion or philanthropy in his head that is not to be questioned, and which spoils all conversation with him. But a friend is a sane man who exercises not my ingenuity, but me. My friend gives me entertainment without requiring any stipulation on my part. A friend, therefore, is a sort of paradox in nature. I who alone am, I who see nothing in nature whose existence I can affirm with equal evidence to my own, behold now the semblance of my being, in all its height, variety, and curiosity, reiterated in a foreign form; so that a friend may well be reckoned the masterpiece of nature.

The other element of friendship is tenderness. We are holden to men by every sort of tie, by blood, by pride, by fear, by hope, by lucre, by lust, by hate, by admiration, by every circumstance and badge and trifle, but we can scarce believe that so much character can subsist in another as to draw us by love. Can another be so blessed, and we so pure, that we can offer him tenderness? When a man becomes dear to me, I have touched the goal of fortune. I find very little written directly to the heart of this matter in books. And yet I have one text which I cannot choose but remember. My author says,— "I offer myself faintly and bluntly to those whose I effectually am, and tender myself least to him to whom I am the most devoted." I wish that friendship should have feet, as well as eyes and eloquence. It must plant itself on the ground, before it vaults over the moon. I wish it to be a little of a citizen, before it is quite a cherub. We chide the citizen because he makes love a commodity. It is an exchange of gifts, of useful loans; it is good neighbourhood; it watches with the sick; it holds the pall at the funeral; and quite loses sight of the delicacies and nobility of the relation. But though we cannot find the god under this disguise of a sutler, yet, on the other hand, we cannot forgive the poet if he spins his thread too fine, and does not substantiate his romance by the municipal virtues of justice, punctuality, fidelity, and pity. I hate the prostitution of the name of friendship to signify modish and worldly alliances. I much prefer the company of ploughboys and tin-peddlers, to the silken and perfumed amity which celebrates its days of encounter by a frivolous display, by rides in a curricle, and dinners at the best taverns. The end of friendship is a commerce the most strict and homely that can be joined; more strict than any of which we have experience. It is for aid and comfort through all the relations and passages of life and death. It is fit for serene days, and graceful gifts, and country rambles, but also for rough roads and hard fare, shipwreck, poverty, and persecution. It keeps company with the sallies of the wit and the trances of religion. We are to dignify to each other the daily needs and offices of man's life, and embellish it by courage, wisdom, and unity. It should never fall into something usual and settled, but should be alert and inventive, and add rhyme and reason to what was drudgery.

Friendship may be said to require natures so rare and costly, each so well tempered and so happily adapted, and withal so circumstanced, (for even in that particular, a poet says, love demands that the parties be altogether paired,) that its satisfaction can very seldom be assured. It cannot subsist in its perfection, say some of those who are learned in this warm lore of the heart, betwixt more than two. I am not quite so strict in my terms, perhaps because I have never known so high a fellowship as others.

FRIENDSHIP IS UNNECESSARY, LIKE PHILOSOPHY, LIKE ART....IT HAS NO SURVIVAL VALUE; RATHER IT IS ONE OF THOSE THINGS THAT GIVE VALUE TO SURVIVAL.

—C. S. Lewis, *The Four Loves*

TIMON OF ATHENS
WILLIAM SHAKESPEARE

Ceremony was but devised at first

To set a gloss on faint deeds,
   hollow welcomes,

Recanting goodness, sorry ere 'tis
   shown;

But where there is true friendship,
   there needs none.

Pray, sit; more welcome are ye to
   my fortunes

Than my fortunes to me.

"IF IT'S VERY PAINFUL FOR YOU TO CRITICIZE YOUR FRIENDS— YOU'RE SAFE IN DOING IT. BUT IF YOU TAKE THE SLIGHTEST PLEASURE IN IT, THAT'S THE TIME TO HOLD YOUR TONGUE."

—Alice Miller

"IF CIVILIZATION
IS TO SURVIVE, WE
MUST CULTIVATE
THE SCIENCE
OF HUMAN
RELATIONSHIPS—
THE ABILITY OF
ALL PEOPLES, OF
ALL KINDS, TO LIVE
TOGETHER, IN THE
SAME WORLD,
AT PEACE."

—Franklin D. Roosevelt

"A QUARREL BETWEEN FRIENDS, WHEN MADE UP, ADDS A NEW TIE TO FRIENDSHIP."

—Saint Francis de Sales

FORGIVENESS

JOHN GREENLEAF WHITTIER

My heart was heavy, for its trust had been
Abused, its kindness answered with foul wrong;
So, turning gloomily from my fellow-men,
One summer Sabbath day I strolled among
The green mounds of the village burial-place;
Where, pondering how all human love and hate
Find one sad level; and how, soon or late,
Wronged and wrongdoer, each with meekened face,
And cold hands folded over a still heart,
Pass the green threshold of our common grave,
Whither all footsteps tend, whence none depart,
Awed for myself, and pitying my race,
Our common sorrow, like a mighty wave,
Swept all my pride away, and trembling I forgave!

A TIME TO TALK

ROBERT FROST

When a friend calls to me from the road
And slows his horse to a meaning walk,
I don't stand still and look around
On all the hills I haven't hoed,
And shout from where I am, What is it?
No, not as there is a time to talk.
I thrust my hoe in the mellow ground,
Blade-end up and five feet tall,
And plod: I go up to the stone wall
For a friendly visit.

"YOU WIN THE VICTORY WHEN YOU YIELD TO FRIENDS."

—Sophocles

"TWO PERSONS CANNOT LONG BE FRIENDS IF THEY CANNOT FORGIVE EACH OTHER'S LITTLE FAILINGS."

—Jean de la Bruyère

NICOMACHEAN ETHICS

ARISTOTLE

There are therefore three kinds of friendship, equal in number to the things that are lovable; for with respect to each there is a mutual and recognized love, and those who love each other wish well to each other in that respect in which they love one another. Now those who love each other for their utility do not love each other for themselves but in virtue of some good which they get from each other. So too with those who love for the sake of pleasure; it is not for their character that men love ready-witted people, but because they find them pleasant. Therefore those who love for the sake of utility love for the sake of what is good for themselves, and those who love for the sake of pleasure do so for the sake of what is pleasant to themselves, and not in so far as the other is the person loved but in so far as he is useful or pleasant. And thus these friendships are only incidental; for it is not as being the man he is that the loved person is loved, but as providing some good or pleasure. Such friendships, then, are easily dissolved, if the parties do not remain like themselves; for if the one party is no longer pleasant or useful the other ceases to love him.

Now the useful is not permanent but is always changing. Thus when the motive of the friendship is done away, the friendship is dissolved, inasmuch as it existed only for the ends in question. This kind of friendship seems to exist chiefly between old people (for at that age people pursue not the pleasant but the useful) and, of those who are in their prime or young, between those who pursue utility. And such people do not live much with each other either; for sometimes they do not even find each other pleasant; therefore they do not need such companionship unless they are useful to each other; for they are pleasant to each other only in so far as they rouse in each other hopes of something good to come. Among such friendships people also class the friendship of a host and guest. On the other hand the friendship of young people seems to aim at pleasure; for they live under the guidance of emotion, and pursue above all what is pleasant to themselves and what is immediately before them; but with increasing age their pleasures become different. This is why they quickly become friends and quickly cease to be so; their friendship changes with the object that is found pleasant, and such pleasure alters quickly. Young people are amorous too; for the greater part of the friendship of love depends on emotion and aims at pleasure; this is why they fall in love and quickly fall out of love, changing often within a single day. But these people do wish to spend their days and lives together; for it is thus that they attain the purpose of their friendship.

Perfect friendship is the friendship of men who are good, and alike in virtue; for these wish well alike to each other qua good, and they are good themselves. Now those who wish well to their friends for their sake are most truly friends; for they do this by reason of own nature and not incidentally; therefore their friendship lasts as long as they are good—and goodness is an enduring thing. And each is good without qualification and to his friend, for the good are both good without qualification and useful to each other. So too they are pleasant; for the good are pleasant both without qualification and to each other, since to each his own activities and others like them are pleasurable, and the actions of the good are the same or like. And such a friendship is as might be expected permanent, since there meet in it all the qualities that friends should have. For all friendship is for the sake of good or of pleasure— good or pleasure either in the abstract or such as will be enjoyed by him who has the friendly feeling—and is based on a certain resemblance; and to a friendship of good men all the qualities we have named belong in virtue of the nature of the friends themselves; for in the case of this kind of friendship the other qualities also are alike in both friends, and that which is good without qualification is also without qualification pleasant, and these are the most lovable qualities. Love and friendship therefore are found most and in their best form between such men.

But it is natural that such friendships should be infrequent; for such men are rare. Further, such friendship requires time and familiarity; as the proverb says, men cannot know each other till they have "eaten salt together"; nor can they admit each other to friendship or be friends till each has been found lovable and been trusted by each. Those who quickly show the marks of friendship to each other wish to be friends, but are not friends unless they both are lovable and know the fact; for a wish for friendship may arise quickly, but friendship does not.

"LOVE AND COMPASSION ARE NECESSITIES, NOT LUXURIES. WITHOUT THEM HUMANITY CANNOT SURVIVE."

—the 14th Dalai Lama

PEACE
BETWEEN
LOVERS

"A LOVING HEART
IS THE TRUEST
WISDOM."

—Charles Dickens

FORGIVENESS

Æ (GEORGE WILLIAM RUSSELL)

AT dusk the window panes grew grey;
The wet world vanished in the gloom;
The dim and silver end of day
Scarce glimmered through the little room.

And all my sins were told; I said
Such things to her who knew not sin—
The sharp ache throbbing in my head,
The fever running high within.

I touched with pain her purity;
Sin's darker sense I could not bring:
My soul was black as night to me;
To her I was a wounded thing.

I needed love no words could say;
She drew me softly nigh her chair,
My head upon her knees to lay,
With cool hands that caressed my hair.

She sat with hands as if to bless,
And looked with grave, ethereal eyes;
Ensouled by ancient Quietness,
A gentle priestess of the Wise.

PEACE

W. B. YEATS

Ah, that Time could touch a form
That could show what Homer's age
Bred to be a hero's wage.
'Were not all her life but storm
Would not painters paint a form
Of such noble lines,' I said,
'Such a delicate high head,
All that sternness amid charm,
All that sweetness amid strength?'
Ah, but peace that comes at length,
Came when Time had touched her form.

"THE CURE FOR ALL THE ILLS AND WRONGS, THE CARES, THE SORROWS, AND THE CRIMES OF HUMANITY, ALL LIE IN THE ONE WORD 'LOVE.' IT IS THE DIVINE VITALITY THAT EVERYWHERE PRODUCES AND RESTORES LIFE."

—Lydia Maria Child

A LETTER
FROM EMMA DARWIN
TO CHARLES DARWIN:

I cannot tell you the compassion I have felt for all your sufferings for these weeks past that you have had so many drawbacks. Nor the gratitude I have felt for the cheerful & affectionate looks you have given me when I know you have been miserably uncomfortable.

My heart has often been too full to speak or take any notice. I am sure you know I love you well enough to believe that I mind your sufferings nearly as much as I should my own & I find the only relief to my own mind is to take it as from God's hand, & to try to believe that all suffering & illness is meant to help us to exalt our minds & to look forward with hope to a future state. When I see your patience, deep compassion for others self command & above all gratitude for the smallest thing done to help you I cannot help longing that these precious feelings should be offered to Heaven for the sake of your daily happiness. But I find it difficult enough in my own case. I often think of the words "Thou shalt keep him in perfect peace whose mind is stayed on thee." It is feeling & not reasoning that drives one to prayer. I feel presumptuous in writing thus to you.

I feel in my inmost heart your admirable qualities & feelings & all I would hope is that you might direct them upwards, as well as to one who values them above every thing in the world. I shall keep this by me till I feel cheerful & comfortable again about you but it has passed through my mind often lately so I thought I would write it partly to relieve my own mind.

"LOVE IS THE CROWNING GRACE OF HUMANITY, THE HOLIEST RIGHT OF THE SOUL, THE GOLDEN LINK WHICH BINDS US TO DUTY AND TRUTH, THE REDEEMING PRINCIPLE THAT CHIEFLY RECONCILES THE HEART TO LIFE, AND IS PROPHETIC OF ETERNAL GOOD."

—Petrarch

"ONE CAN GIVE WITHOUT LOVING, BUT ONE CANNOT LOVE WITHOUT GIVING."

—Amy Carmichael

CONSTANCY TO AN IDEAL OBJECT

SAMUEL TAYLOR COLERIDGE

Since all that beat about in Nature's range,

Or veer or vanish; why should'st thou remain

The only constant in a world of change,

O yearning Thought! that liv'st but in the brain?

Call to the Hours, that in the distance play,

The faery people of the future day—

Fond Thought! not one of all that shining swarm

Will breathe on thee with life-enkindling breath,

Till when, like strangers shelt'ring from a storm,

Hope and Despair meet in the porch of Death!

Yet still thou haunt'st me; and though well I see,

She is not thou, and only thou are she,

Still, still as though some dear embodied Good,

Some living Love before my eyes there stood

With answering look a ready ear to lend,

I mourn to thee and say—'Ah! loveliest friend!

That this the meed of all my toils might be,

To have a home, an English home, and thee!'

Vain repetition! Home and Thou are one.

The peacefull'st cot, the moon shall shine upon,
Lulled by the thrush and wakened by the lark,
Without thee were but a becalméd bark,
Whose Helmsman on an ocean waste and wide
Sits mute and pale his mouldering helm beside.

And art thou nothing? Such thou art, as when
The woodman winding westward up the glen
At wintry dawn, where o'er the sheep-track's maze
The viewless snow-mist weaves a glist'ning haze,
Sees full before him, gliding without tread,
An image with a glory round its head;
The enamoured rustic worships its fair hues,
Nor knows he makes the shadow, he pursues!

EXCERPT FROM
SENSE AND SENSIBILITY
JANE AUSTEN

When he was present she had no eyes for anyone else. Everything he did was right. Everything he said was clever. If their evenings at the park were concluded with cards, he cheated himself and all the rest of the party to get her a good hand. If dancing formed the amusement of the night, they were partners for half the time; and when obliged to separate for a couple of dances, were careful to stand together and scarcely spoke a word to anyone else. Such conduct made them, of course, most exceedingly laughed at; but ridicule could not shame and seemed hardly to provoke them.

LOVE SOUGHT IS GOOD, BUT GIVEN UNSOUGHT, IS BETTER.

—William Shakespeare, *Twelfth Night*

"THE BEST AND MOST BEAUTIFUL THINGS IN THIS WORLD CANNOT BE SEEN OR EVEN TOUCHED. THEY MUST BE FELT WITH THE HEART."

—Helen Keller

SONGS ABOUT FIGHTING FOR PEACE IN A RELATIONSHIP

Ordinary People: **John Legend**

Let's Stay Together: **Al Green**

Happy Together: **The Turtles**

We Can Do Better: **Matt Simons**

Kiss and Make Up: **Dua Lipa & BLACKPINK**

Please Forgive Me: **Bryan Adams**

I Won't Give Up: **Jason Mraz**

You're Still the One: **Shania Twain**

Bless the Broken Road: **Rascal Flatts**

Just Give Me a Reason: **Pink & Nate Ruess**

Remind Me: **Brad Paisley & Carrie Underwood**

NEAR THE CASCADES

AMEEN RIHANI

Hold back thy lips, I pray;
Just let me rest this way;
My soul is in the spray
Arising from the silvery cascades murmuring
farewell to the day.

Thy kisses 'neath a sigh
Of mine extinguished lie;
O friend, I choke, I die:
Pray, let me raise my head to see the parting
Light, the vivid sky,

If every kiss of thine
Is safety kept with mine
For one for whom I pine,
Wouldst thou, contented with the taking, call my
love a love divine?

Ay, and for every tear
Thou sheddest when I'm near
I shed a score to hear
Her echo my desire's sigh, albeit she is not thy
peer.

If I were but a reed,
Or but a fern or weed,
This would not be my creed;
But prick thou these cold slips and all the roots
of me in heaven will bleed.

Thy burning breath is creeping
All over me; 't is leaping
Into my bones and sweeping
Their ashes out, up and into mine eyes, alas!
    the awful reaping.

No longer do I fear,
Nor see, nor feel, nor hear;
No longer am I near;
If thou wilt quench thy flame, kiss now the lips
    that were to thee so dear.

As well kiss thou the grass
On which I lay, alas!
Like me, thou too wilt pass;
One kiss will turn thy lips to ashes and one tear,
    thine eyes to glass.

Beneath this hemlock tree
A clod I leave to thee;
But over land and sea
My soul is rising, rising, rising, searching for the
    gods that be.

But gods have lived, and lied,
And loved, and fell, and died;
And like me too they cried
For mercy at the snow white feet of Beauty's
    daughter,
        Beauty's bride.

And when from Beauty's spell
Her soul is free, she'll dwell
In mine, the storm to quell;
In mine she'll rise to realms of bliss, or swiftly
    whirl into the deepest hell.

YOUTH INSATIATE

ELSA GIDLOW

If I have wished for skies unscarred by storm,
Shrunk from the grievous bitterness of things,
The days' perplexities, the nights' unrest,
The cruel, fruitless beating with clipped wings

Against the windows of the Infinite,
And, weary with the conflict's puerile stress,
Cried out against it all, cried out for peace,
Even what peace the rotting dead possess,

May Life forgive me: I am stronger now,
The play bewilders, but I know my part;
And I have learned that Beauty is salt blood
Pain-wrung from the unconquerable heart.

Let there be laughter then, love's wine and bread,
The many mouths of passion, their joys, their grief;
These are but soil and seed—for what grave growths?
I plant and wait, (and pray the time be brief!)

Lean wisdom this, to pause and taste and pause
Like a scared virgin who must stop for breath.
Take the cup simply, drain it to the lees;
Then, smiling, fling the empty cup to Death.

"YOU WILL FIND AS YOU LOOK BACK UPON YOUR LIFE THAT THE MOMENTS WHEN YOU HAVE TRULY LIVED ARE THE MOMENTS WHEN YOU HAVE DONE THINGS IN THE SPIRIT OF LOVE."

—Henry Drummond

"LOVE IS THE ONLY REALITY AND IT IS NOT A MERE SENTIMENT. IT IS THE ULTIMATE TRUTH THAT LIES AT THE HEART OF CREATION."

—Rabindranath Tagore

THE LOVER ASKS FORGIVENESS BECAUSE OF HIS MANY MOODS

W. B. YEATS

If this importunate heart trouble your peace
With words lighter than air,
Or hopes that in mere hoping flicker and cease;
Crumple the rose in your hair;
And cover your lips with odorous twilight and say,
'O Hearts of wind-blown flame!
O Winds, older than changing of night and day,
That murmuring and longing came
From marble cities loud with tabors of old
In dove-grey faery lands;
From battle-banners, fold upon purple fold,
Queens wrought with glimmering hands;
That saw young Niamh hover with love-lorn face
Above the wandering tide;
And lingered in the hidden desolate place
Where the last Phoenix died,
And wrapped the flames above his holy head;
And still murmur and long:
O piteous Hearts, changing till change be dead
In a tumultuous song':
And cover the pale blossoms of your breast
With your dim heavy hair,
And trouble with a sigh for all things longing for rest
The odorous twilight there.

LES MISÉRABLES
VICTOR HUGO

The future belongs to hearts even more than it does to minds. Love, that is the only thing that can occupy and fill eternity. In the infinite, the inexhaustible is requisite.

Love participates of the soul itself. It is of the same nature. Like it, it is the divine spark; like it, it is incorruptible, indivisible, imperishable. It is a point of fire that exists within us, which is immortal and infinite, which nothing can confine, and which nothing can extinguish.

Oh Love! Adorations! voluptuousness of two minds which understand each other, of two hearts which exchange with each other, of two glances which penetrate each other! You will come to me, will you not, bliss! strolls by twos in the solitudes! Blessed and radiant days! I have sometimes dreamed that from time to time hours detached themselves from the lives of the angels and came here below to traverse the destinies of men.

God can add nothing to the happiness of those who love, except to give them endless duration. God is the plenitude of heaven; love is the plenitude of man.

I MUST LEARN TO BE CONTENT WITH BEING HAPPIER THAN I DESERVE.

—Jane Austen, *Pride and Prejudice*

PEACE
BETWEEN
ENEMIES

"PEACE IS THE ONLY BATTLE WORTH WAGING."

—Albert Camus

THE DIVINE IMAGE

WILLIAM BLAKE

To Mercy, Pity, Peace, and Love,
All pray in their distress:
And to these virtues of delight
Return their thankfulness.

For Mercy, Pity, Peace, and Love,
Is God, our father dear:
And Mercy, Pity, Peace, and Love,
Is Man, his child and care.

For Mercy has a human heart,
Pity, a human face:
And Love, the human form divine,
And Peace, the human dress.

Then every man of every clime,
That prays in his distress,
Prays to the human form divine,
Love, Mercy, Pity, Peace.

And all must love the human form,
In heathen, Turk, or Jew.
Where Mercy, Love, and Pity dwell,
There God is dwelling too.

"MAN MUST EVOLVE FOR ALL HUMAN CONFLICT A METHOD WHICH REJECTS REVENGE, AGGRESSION, AND RETALIATION. THE FOUNDATION OF SUCH A METHOD IS LOVE."

—Martin Luther King Jr.

"HATRED DOES NOT CEASE BY HATRED, BUT ONLY BY LOVE; THIS IS THE ETERNAL RULE."

—Guatama Buddha

1953 ATOMS FOR PEACE SPEECH

AT THE 470TH PLENARY MEETING OF THE UNITED NATIONS GENERAL ASSEMBLY

DWIGHT D. EISENHOWER

Should such an atomic attack be launched against the United States, our reactions would be swift and resolute. But for me to say that the defense capabilities of the United States are such that they could inflict terrible losses upon an aggressor—for me to say that the retaliation capabilities of the United States are so great that such an aggressor's land would be laid waste—all this, while fact, is not the true expression of the purpose and the hope of the United States.

To pause there would be to confirm the hopeless finality of a belief that two atomic colossi are doomed malevolently to eye each other indefinitely across a trembling world. To stop there would be to accept helplessly the probability of civilization destroyed—the annihilation of the irreplaceable heritage of mankind handed down to us from generation to generation—and the condemnation of mankind to begin all over again the age-old struggle upward from savagery toward decency, and right, and justice.

Surely no sane member of the human race could discover victory in such desolation. Could anyone wish his name to be coupled by history with such human degradation and destruction.

Occasional pages of history do record the faces of the "Great Destroyers" but the whole book of history reveals mankind's never-ending quest for peace, and mankind's God-given capacity to build.

It is with the book of history, and not with isolated pages, that the United States will ever wish to be identified. My country wants to be constructive, not destructive. It wants agreements, not wars, among nations. It wants itself to live in freedom, and in the confidence that the people of every other nation enjoy equally the right of choosing their own way of life.

So my country's purpose is to help us move out of the dark chamber of horrors into the light, to find a way by which the minds of men, the hopes of men, the souls of men everywhere, can move forward toward peace and happiness and well-being.

In this quest, I know that we must not lack patience. I know that in a world divided, such as ours today, salvation cannot be attained by one dramatic act. I know that many steps will have to be taken over many months before the world can look at itself one day and truly realize that a new climate of mutually peaceful confidence is abroad in the world. But I know, above all else, that we must start to take these steps—now.

"PEACE CANNOT BE KEPT BY FORCE, IT CAN ONLY BE ACHIEVED BY UNDERSTANDING."

—Albert Einstein

MINE ENEMY IS GROWING OLD

EMILY DICKINSON

Mine Enemy is growing old—

I have at last Revenge—

The Palate of the Hate departs—

If any would avenge

Let him be quick—the Viand flits—

It is a faded Meat—

Anger as soon as fed is dead—

'Tis starving makes it fat—

"ANGER IS AN ACID THAT CAN DO MORE HARM TO THE VESSEL IN WHICH IT IS STORED THAN TO ANYTHING ON WHICH IT IS POURED."

—Mark Twain

NO MAN CHOOSES EVIL BECAUSE IT IS EVIL; HE ONLY MISTAKES IT FOR HAPPINESS, THE GOOD HE SEEKS.

—Mary Wollstonecraft,
A Vindication of the Rights of Men

"LOVE IS THE ONLY FORCE CAPABLE OF TRANSFORMING AN ENEMY INTO A FRIEND."

—Martin Luther King Jr.

I WAKE AND FEEL THE FELL OF DARK, NOT DAY

GERARD MANLEY HOPKINS

I wake and feel the fell of dark, not day.
What hours, O what black hours we have spent
This night! what sights you, heart, saw; ways you went!
And more must, in yet longer light's delay.

With witness I speak this. But where I say
Hours I mean years, mean life. And my lament
Is cries countless, cries like dead letters sent
To dearest him that lives alas! away.

I am gall, I am heartburn. God's most deep decree
Bitter would have me taste: my taste was me;
Bones built in me, flesh filled, blood brimmed the curse.

Selfyeast of spirit a dull dough sours. I see
The lost are like this, and their scourge to be
As I am mine, their sweating selves, but worse.

FINAL REMARKS AS FIRST LADY

MICHELLE OBAMA

If you are a person of faith, know that religious diversity is a great American tradition too. In fact, that's why people first came to this country—to worship freely. And whether you are Muslim, Christian, Jewish, Hindu, Sikh — these religions are teaching our young people about justice, and compassion, and honesty. So I want our young people to continue to learn and practice those values with pride. You see, our glorious diversity—our diversities of faiths and colors and creeds—that is not a threat to who we are, it makes us who we are. So the young people here and the young people out there: do not ever let anyone make you feel like you don't matter, or like you don't have a place in our American story—because you do. And you have a right to be exactly who you are. But I also want to be very clear: this right isn't just handed to you. No, this right has to be earned every single day. You cannot take your freedoms for granted. Just like generations who have come before you, you have to do your part to preserve and protect those freedoms. And that starts right now, when you're young.

Right now, you need to be preparing yourself to add your voice to our national conversation. You need to prepare yourself to be informed and engaged as a citizen, to serve and to lead, to stand up for our proud American values and to honor them in your daily lives. And that means getting the best education possible so you can think critically, so you can express yourself clearly, so you can get a good job and support yourself and your family, so you can be a positive force in your communities.

And when you encounter obstacles—because I guarantee you, you will, and many of you already have—when you are struggling and you start thinking about giving up, I want you to remember something that my husband and I have talked about since we first started this journey nearly a decade ago, something that has carried us through every moment in this White House and every moment of our lives, and that is the power of hope—the belief that something better is always possible if you're willing to work for it and fight for it.

It is our fundamental belief in the power of hope that has allowed us to rise above the voices of doubt and division, of anger and fear that we have faced in our own lives and in the life of this country. Our hope that if we work hard enough and believe in ourselves, then we can be whatever we dream, regardless of the limitations that others may place on us. The hope that when people see us for who we truly are, maybe, just maybe, they too will be inspired to rise to their best possible selves.

That is the hope of students like Kyra who fight to discover their gifts and share them with the world. It's the hope of school counselors like Terri and all these folks up here who guide those students every step of the way, refusing to give up on even a single young person. Shoot, it's the hope of my—folks like my dad who got up every day to do his job at the city water plant; the hope that one day, his kids would go to college and have opportunities he never dreamed of.

That's the kind of hope that every single one of us—politicians, parents, preachers—all of us need to be providing for our young people. Because that is what moves this country forward every single day—our hope for the future and the hard work that hope inspires.

CORRUPTION WINS NOT MORE THAN HONESTY. STILL IN THY RIGHT HAND CARRY GENTLE PEACE, TO SILENCE ENVIOUS TONGUES.

—William Shakespeare, *Henry VIII*

"THOSE WHO
ARE AT WAR WITH
OTHERS ARE NOT
AT PEACE WITH
THEMSELVES."

—William Hazlitt

GOOD-BYE

RALPH WALDO EMERSON

Good-bye, proud world! I'm going home:
Thou art not my friend, and I'm not thine.
Long through thy weary crowds I roam;
A river-ark on the ocean brine,
Long I've been tossed like the driven foam;
But now, proud world! I'm going home.

Good-bye to Flattery's fawning face;
To Grandeur with his wise grimace;
To upstart Wealth's averted eye;
To supple Office, low and high;
To crowded halls, to court and street;
To frozen hearts and hasting feet;
To those who go, and those who come;
Good-bye, proud world! I'm going home.

I am going to my own hearth-stone,
Bosomed in yon green hills alone, —
A secret nook in a pleasant land,
Whose groves the frolic fairies planned;
Where arches green, the livelong day,
Echo the blackbird's roundelay,
And vulgar feet have never trod
A spot that is sacred to thought and God.

O, when I am safe in my sylvan home,
I tread on the pride of Greece and Rome;
And when I am stretched beneath the pines,
Where the evening star so holy shines,
I laugh at the lore and the pride of man,
At the sophist schools, and the learned clan;
For what are they all, in their high conceit,
When man in the bush with God may meet?

"IT IS EASIER TO FORGIVE AN ENEMY THAN TO FORGIVE A FRIEND."

—William Blake

"THE WEAK CAN NEVER FORGIVE. FORGIVENESS IS THE ATTRIBUTE OF THE STRONG."

—Mahatma Gandhi

"IT IS IN PARDONING THAT WE ARE PARDONED."

—Saint Francis of Assisi

THE MAN HE KILLED

THOMAS HARDY

"Had he and I but met
      By some old ancient inn,
We should have sat us down to wet
      Right many a nipperkin!

"But ranged as infantry,
      And staring face to face,
I shot at him as he at me,
      And killed him in his place.

"I shot him dead because—
      Because he was my foe,
Just so: my foe of course he was;
      That's clear enough; although

"He thought he'd 'list, perhaps,
      Off-hand like—just as I—
Was out of work—had sold his traps—
      No other reason why.

"Yes; quaint and curious war is!
      You shoot a fellow down
You'd treat if met where any bar is,
      Or help to half-a-crown."

SPRING OFFENSIVE

WILFRED OWEN

Halted against the shade of a last hill,
They fed, and, lying easy, were at ease
And, finding comfortable chests and knees
Carelessly slept.
              But many there stood still
To face the stark, blank sky beyond the ridge,
Knowing their feet had come to the end of the world.
Marvelling they stood, and watched the long grass
   swirled
By the May breeze, murmurous with wasp and midge,
For though the summer oozed into their veins
Like the injected drug for their bones' pains,
Sharp on their souls hung the imminent line of grass,
Fearfully flashed the sky's mysterious glass.

Hour after hour they ponder the warm field—
And the far valley behind, where the buttercups
Had blessed with gold their slow boots coming up,
Where even the little brambles would not yield,
But clutched and clung to them like sorrowing hands;
They breathe like trees unstirred.
Till like a cold gust thrilled the little word
At which each body and its soul begird
And tighten them for battle. No alarms
Of bugles, no high flags, no clamorous haste—
Only a lift and flare of eyes that faced
The sun, like a friend with whom their love is done.

O larger shone that smile against the sun,—
Mightier than his whose bounty these have spurned.

So, soon they topped the hill, and raced together
Over an open stretch of herb and heather
Exposed. And instantly the whole sky burned
With fury against them; and soft sudden cups
Opened in thousands for their blood; and the green
    slopes
Chasmed and steepened sheer to infinite space.

Of them who running on that last high place
Leapt to swift unseen bullets, or went up
On the hot blast and fury of hell's upsurge,
Or plunged and fell away past this world's verge,
Some say God caught them even before they fell.
But what say such as from existence' brink
Ventured but drave too swift to sink.
The few who rushed in the body to enter hell,
And there out-fiending all its fiends and flames
With superhuman inhumanities,
Long-famous glories, immemorial shames—
And crawling slowly back, have by degrees
Regained cool peaceful air in wonder—
Why speak they not of comrades that went under?

SWEET MERCY IS NOBILITY'S TRUE BADGE.

—William Shakespeare, *Titus Andronicus*

"DO I NOT DESTROY MY ENEMIES WHEN I MAKE THEM MY FRIENDS?"

—Abraham Lincoln

WORLD
PEACE

"PEACE IS NOT
THE ABSENCE
OF CONFLICT,
BUT THE ABILITY
TO COPE WITH
CONFLICT
BY PEACEFUL
MEANS."

—Ronald Reagan

"TEAR DOWN THIS WALL" SPEECH

RONALD REAGAN

We welcome change and openness; for we believe that freedom and security go together, that the advance of human liberty can only strengthen the cause of world peace. There is one sign the Soviets can make that would be unmistakable, that would advance dramatically the cause of freedom and peace.

General Secretary Gorbachev, if you seek peace, if you seek prosperity for the Soviet Union and Eastern Europe, if you seek liberalization: come here to this gate! Mr. Gorbachev, open this gate! Mr. Gorbachev, tear down this wall!

COUNTING, THIS NEW YEAR'S MORNING, WHAT POWERS YET REMAIN TO ME

JANE HIRSHFIELD

The world asks, as it asks daily:
*And what can you make, can you do, to change my deep
 broken, fractured?*

I count, this first day of another year, what remains.
I have a mountain, a kitchen, two hands.

Can admire with two eyes the mountain,
actual, recalcitrant, shuffling its pebbles, sheltering foxes and
 beetles.

Can make black-eyed peas and collards.
Can make, from last year's late-ripening persimmons, a
 pudding.

Can climb a stepladder, change the bulb in a track light.

For four years, I woke each day first to the mountain,
then to the question.

The feet of the new sufferings followed the feet of the old,
and still they surprised.

I brought salt, brought oil, to the question. Brought sweet tea,
brought postcards and stamps. For four years, each day,
   something.

Stone did not become apple. War did not become peace.
Yet joy still stays joy. Sequins stay sequins. Words still
   bespangle, bewilder.

Today, I woke without answer.

The day answers, unpockets a thought from a friend

don't despair of this falling world, not yet

didn't it give you the asking

JOHN F. KENNEDY

Let us examine our attitude toward peace itself. Too many of us think it is impossible. Too many think it unreal. But that is a dangerous, defeatist belief. It leads to the conclusion that war is inevitable—that mankind is doomed—that we are gripped by forces we cannot control.

We need not accept that view. Our problems are man-made—therefore, they can be solved by man. And man can be as big as he wants. No problem of human destiny is beyond human beings. Man's reason and spirit have often solved the seemingly unsolvable—and we believe they can do it again.

I am not referring to the absolute, infinite concept of peace and goodwill of which some fantasies and fanatics dream. I do not deny the value of hopes and dreams but we merely invite discouragement and incredulity by making that our only and immediate goal.

Let us focus instead on a more practical, more attainable peace—based not on a sudden revolution in human nature but on a gradual evolution in human institutions—on a series of concrete actions and effective agreements which are in the interest of all concerned. There is no single, simple key to this peace—no grand or magic formula to be adopted by one or two powers. Genuine peace must be the product of many nations, the sum of many acts. It must be dynamic, not static, changing to meet the challenge of each new generation. For peace is a process—a way of solving problems.

With such a peace, there will still be quarrels and conflicting interests, as there are within families and nations. World peace, like community peace, does not require that each man love his neighbor—it requires only that they live together in mutual tolerance, submitting their disputes to a just and peaceful settlement. And history teaches us that enmities between nations, as between individuals, do not last forever. However fixed our likes and dislikes may seem, the tide of time and events will often bring surprising changes in the relations between nations and neighbors.

So let us persevere. Peace need not be impracticable, and war need not be inevitable. By defining our goal more clearly, by making it seem more manageable and less remote, we can help all peoples to see it, to draw hope from it, and to move irresistibly toward it.

"WHILE YOU ARE PROCLAIMING PEACE WITH YOUR LIPS, BE CAREFUL TO HAVE IT EVEN MORE FULLY IN YOUR HEART."

—Saint Francis of Assisi

"IT ISN'T ENOUGH
TO TALK ABOUT
PEACE. ONE MUST
BELIEVE IN IT. AND
IT ISN'T ENOUGH
TO BELIEVE IN IT.
ONE MUST WORK
AT IT."

—Eleanor Roosevelt

CHRISTMAS SERMON

IN ATLANTA, GEORGIA, 1967

MARTIN LUTHER KING JR.

If we are to have peace on Earth, our loyalties must become ecumenical rather than sectional. Our loyalties must transcend our race, our tribe, our class, and our nation; and this means we must develop a world perspective.

"AN INGLORIOUS
PEACE IS
BETTER THAN A
DISHONORABLE WAR."

—Mark Twain

EXCERPT FROM
"ADDRESS ON WOMAN'S RIGHTS"
(SEPTEMBER 1948)

ELIZABETH CADY STANTON

Now is the time, now emphatically, for the women of this country to buckle on the armor that can best resist the weapons of the enemy, ridicule and holy horror. "Voices" were the visitors and advisers of Joan of Arc, "voices" have come to us, oftimes from the depths of sorrow degradation and despair—they have been too long unheeded. The same religious enthusiasm that nerved her to what she deemed her work now nerves us to ours, her work was prophesied of, ours too is the fulfilling of what has long since been foretold. In the better days your sons and your daughters shall prophesy. Her struggle and triumph were alike short, our struggle shall be hard and long but our triumph shall be complete and forever. We do not expect that our path will be strewn with the flowers of popular favour—that our banner which we have flung to the wind will be fanned by the breath of popular applause, no we know that over the nettles of prejudice and bigotry will be our way, that upon our banner will beat the dark stormcloud of opposition from those who have entrenched themselves behind the strong bulwark of might, of force and who have fortified their position by every means holy and unholy, but we steadfastly abide the result. Unmoved we will bear it aloft-undaunted we will unfurl it to the gal—we know the storm cannot rend from it a shred, that the electric flash will but more clearly show to us the glorious words inscribed upon it, "Equality of rights" and the rolling thunder will be sweet music in our ears, telling us of the light [rest of line torn away] of the purer clearer atmosphere [rest of line torn away].

A new era is dawn[ing upon the world,] when old might to right [must yield the battle blade] to clerkly pen, when the m[illions] now under the iron heel of [the ty-rant will assert] their manhood, when woman [yielding to the] voice of the spirit within her will [demand the] recognition of her humanity, when [her soul, grown] too large for her chains, will burst th[e bands] around her set and stand redeemed regenerated and disenthralled.

PEACE IS ALWAYS BEAUTIFUL.

—Walt Whitman, *The Sleepers*

THE GIFT OF INDIA

SAROJINI NAIDU

Is there aught you need that my hands withhold,
Rich gifts of raiment or grain or gold?
Lo! I have flung to the East and West
Priceless treasures torn from my breast,
And yielded the sons of my stricken womb
To the drum-beats of duty, the sabres of doom.

Gathered like pearls in their alien graves
Silent they sleep by the Persian waves,
Scattered like shells on Egyptian sands,
They lie with pale brows and brave, broken hands,
They are strewn like blossoms mown down by chance
On the blood-brown meadows of Flanders and France.

Can ye measure the grief of the tears I weep
Or compass the woe of the watch I keep?
Or the pride that thrills thro' my heart's despair
And the hope that comforts the anguish of prayer?
And the far sad glorious vision I see
Of the torn red banners of Victory?

When the terror and tumult of hate shall cease
And life be refashioned on anvils of peace,
And your love shall offer memorial thanks
To the comrades who fought in your dauntless ranks,
And you honour the deeds of the deathless ones
Remember the blood of thy martyred sons!

FIRST SUPPLEMENT: OF THE GUARANTEE OF PERPETUAL PEACE

IMMANUEL KANT

The guarantee of Perpetual Peace is furnished by no less a power than the great artist Nature herself: *Natura Daedala rerum*. The mechanical course of Nature visibly exhibits a design to bring forth concord out of the discord of men, even against their will. This power as a cause working by laws which are unknown to us, is commonly called Fate; but in view of the design manifested in the course of the world, it is to be regarded as the deep wisdom of a Higher Cause directed towards the realization of the final purpose of the human race, and predetermining the course of the world by relation to it, and as such we call it Providence. This power we do not indeed perceive externally in the artistic formations of Nature, nor can we even infer from them to it; but as in all referring of the form of things to final causes generally, we not only can, but must conjoin this thought with them in order to make their possibility conceivable after the analogy of the operations of human art. The relation and accord of these things to the moral purpose which reason immediately prescribes to us, can only be represented by an idea which theoretically indeed transcends our experience, but which is practically determinable and is well founded in reality. Such for example is the idea of a Perpetual Peace being a duty when the mechanism of nature is regarded as conducing to its realization. The employment of the term 'Nature' rather than 'Providence' for the designation of this power, is more proper and more modest in view of the limits of human reason, when we are dealing with it merely from the theoretical and not from the religious point of view. For human reason, when dealing with the relation of effects to their causes, must keep within the limits of possible experience; and to speak of Providence as knowable by us in this relation, would be putting on Icarian wings with presumptuous rashness in order to approach the mystery of His unfathomable purposes.

Before determining this guarantee more exactly, it will be necessary to look first at that state of things arranged by nature for those who live and act upon the stage of her great theatre, which ultimately gives the guarantee of Peace. Thereafter we shall consider the manner in which this guarantee is furnished. The provisory arrangements of nature in this relation consist mainly in these three things: 1st, she has provided so that men shall be able to live in all parts of the earth; 2nd, she has scattered them everywhere by means of war so that they might populate even the most inhospitable regions; and 3rd, by this same means she has compelled them to enter into relations more or less rightful with one another. The facts that come here into view are truly wonderful. Thus in the cold, icy wastes around the Arctic Ocean there grows the moss which the reindeer scrapes forth from beneath the snow in order that it may itself become food, or that it may be yoked to the sledge of the Ostiak or the Samojan. And in like manner, the wildernesses of sand, barren though they be, do yet contain the camel which appears to have been created for travelling through them, in order that they might not be left unutilized. Still more distinctly does design appear when we come to know how, along with the fur-clad animals on the shores of the Arctic Ocean, there are seals, walruses and whales that furnish food by their flesh, and warmth and light by their fat to the inhabitants around. But most of all does the provident care of nature excite our admiration by the driftwood which it brings to the treeless shores, even when it is not well known whence it comes; and yet without this material the dwellers in the region could neither construct their canoes, nor their arms, nor huts for their abode; and this too under such conditions as compel them to carry on war against the wild beasts, so that they have to live at peace with each other. Moreover, it is remarkable that it was probably nothing but war that drove men into different regions....

War, however, requires no special motive for its explanation; it appears to be ingrafted on human nature and is even regarded as noble in itself, man being stimulated to it by the love of glory without regard to selfish interests....An inherent dignity was thus attached to war itself, so that even philosophers have glorified it as giving a certain nobleness to humanity, unmindful of the Greek saying that 'war is bad in that it makes more bad people than it takes away.' So much then in reference to what nature does in carrying out her own design in regard to the Human Race as a class of her creatures.

The question then arises, as to what is the essential meaning and aim of this design of a Perpetual Peace. It may be put thus: 'What does Nature do in this respect with reference to the end which man's own reason presents to him as a duty; and, consequently, what does she do for the furtherance of his moral purpose in life? And, further, how does she guarantee that what man ought to do according to the laws of his freedom, and yet does not do, shall be done by him without prejudice to his freedom even by a certain constraint of nature; and how does she secure this in all the three relationships of Public Right as Political Right, International Right and Cosmopolitan Right?' When I say of nature that she *wills* a certain thing to be done, I do not mean that she imposes upon us a duty to do it, for only the Practical Reason as essentially free from constraint, can do this; but I mean that she does it herself whether we be willing or not. 'Fata volentem ducunt, nolentem trahunt'....

In this way Nature guarantees the conditions of Perpetual Peace by the mechanism involved in our human inclinations themselves; and although this is not realized with a guarantee that is sufficient to enable us to *prophesy* the future theoretically, yet the security involved is sufficient for all practical relations. And thus it becomes a duty to labor for the realization of this purpose as not at all chimerical in itself.

"AN ARMY OF PRINCIPLES CAN PENETRATE WHERE AN ARMY OF SOLDIERS CANNOT."

—Thomas Paine

"COURAGE IS THE PRICE THAT LIFE EXACTS FOR GRANTING PEACE."

—Amelia Earhart

SONGS ABOUT WORLD PEACE

Imagine: **John Lennon**

Blowin' in the Wind: **Bob Dylan**

A Change Is Gonna Come: **Sam Cooke**

All You Need Is Love: **The Beatles**

Heal the World: **Michael Jackson**

I Wish You Peace: **Eagles**

Waiting on the World to Change: **John Mayer**

Pipes of Peace: **Paul McCartney**

Get Along: **Kenny Chesney**

Alright: **Kendrick Lamar**

One Day: **Matisyahu**

What's Going On: **Marvin Gaye**

Man of Peace: **Grateful Dead and Bob Dylan**

Peacekeeper: **Fleetwood Mac**

We Are the World: **U.S.A. for Africa**

Give Me Love (Give Me Peace on Earth): **George Harrison**

(What's So Funny 'Bout) Peace, Love and Understanding:
Elvis Costello & the Attractions

Holiday: **Green Day**

Peace Train: **Cat Stevens**

One Love/People Get Ready: **Bob Marley and the Wailers**

Where Is the Love?: **Black Eyed Peas**

Why Can't We Be Friends?: **War**

PEACE

GEORGE HERBERT

Sweet Peace, where dost thou dwell? I humbly crave,
Let me once know.
I sought thee in a secret cave,
And ask'd, if Peace were there.
A hollow wind did seem to answer, No:
Go, seek elsewhere.

I did; and going did a rainbow note:
Surely, thought I,
This is the lace of Peace's coat.
I will search out the matter.
But while I looked the clouds immediately
Did break and scatter.

Then went I to a garden and did spy
A gallant flower,
The crown-imperial: Sure, said I,
Peace at the root must dwell.
But when I digged, I saw a worm devour
What showed so well.

At length I met a rev'rend, good old man;
Whom when for Peace
I did demand, he thus began:
There was a prince of old
At Salem dwelt, who lived with good increase
Of flock and fold.

He sweetly lived; yet sweetness did not save
His life from foes.
But after death out of his grave
There sprang twelve stalks of wheat;
Which many wond'ring at, got some of those
To plant and set.

It prospered strangely, and did soon disperse
Through all the earth:
For they that taste it do rehearse,
That virtue lies therein;
A secret virtue, bringing peace and mirth,
By flight of sin.

Take of this grain, which in my garden grows,
And grows for you;
Make bread of it: and that repose
And peace, which ev'ry where
With so much earnestness you do pursue,
Is only there.

NO ONE IS BORN
HATING ANOTHER
PERSON BECAUSE
OF THE COLOR OF
HIS SKIN, OR HIS
BACKGROUND,
OR HIS RELIGION.
PEOPLE MUST LEARN
TO HATE, AND IF
THEY CAN LEARN TO
HATE, THEY CAN BE
TAUGHT TO LOVE, FOR
LOVE COMES MORE
NATURALLY TO THE
HUMAN HEART THAN
ITS OPPOSITE.

—Nelson Mandela, *Long Walk to Freedom*

MEMORIAL ADDRESS FOR NELSON MANDELA

BARACK OBAMA

For the people of South Africa, for those he inspired around the globe, Madiba's passing is rightly a time of mourning, and a time to celebrate a heroic life. But I believe it should also prompt in each of us a time for self-reflection. With honesty, regardless of our station or our circumstance, we must ask: How well have I applied his lessons in my own life? It's a question I ask myself, as a man and as a President.

We know that, like South Africa, the United States had to overcome centuries of racial subjugation. As was true here, it took sacrifice—the sacrifice of countless people, known and unknown, to see the dawn of a new day. Michelle and I are beneficiaries of that struggle. But in America, and in South Africa, and in countries all around the globe, we cannot allow our progress to cloud the fact that our work is not yet done.

The struggles that follow the victory of formal equality or universal franchise may not be as filled with drama and moral clarity as those that came before, but they are no less important. For around the world today, we still see children suffering from hunger and disease. We still see run-down schools. We still see young people without prospects for the future. Around the world today, men and women are still imprisoned for their political beliefs, and are still persecuted for what they look like, and how they worship, and who they love. That is happening today.

And so we, too, must act on behalf of justice. We, too, must act on behalf of peace. There are too many people who happily embrace Madiba's legacy of racial reconciliation, but passionately resist even modest reforms that would challenge chronic poverty and growing inequality. There are too many leaders who claim solidarity with Madiba's struggle for freedom, but do not tolerate dissent from their own people. And there are too many of us on the sidelines, comfortable in complacency or cynicism when our voices must be heard.

The questions we face today—how to promote equality and justice; how to uphold freedom and human rights; how to end conflict and sectarian war—these things do not have easy answers. But there were no easy answers in front of that child born in World War I. Nelson Mandela reminds us that it always seems impossible until it is done. South Africa shows that is true. South Africa shows we can change, that we can choose a world defined not by our differences, but by our common hopes. We can choose a world defined not by conflict, but by peace and justice and opportunity.

We will never see the likes of Nelson Mandela again. But let me say to the young people of Africa and the young people around the world—you, too, can make his life's work your own. Over 30 years ago, while still a student, I learned of Nelson Mandela and the struggles taking place in this beautiful land, and it stirred something in me. It woke me up to my responsibilities to others and to myself, and it set me on an improbable journey that finds me here today. And while I will always fall short of Madiba's example, he makes me want to be a better man. He speaks to what's best inside us.

After this great liberator is laid to rest, and when we have returned to our cities and villages and rejoined our daily routines, let us search for his strength. Let us search for his largeness of spirit somewhere inside of ourselves. And when the night grows dark, when injustice weighs heavy on our hearts, when our best-laid plans seem beyond our reach, let us think of Madiba and the words that brought him comfort within the four walls of his cell: "It matters not how strait the gate, how charged with punishments the scroll, I am the master of my fate: I am the captain of my soul."

What a magnificent soul it was. We will miss him deeply. May God bless the memory of Nelson Mandela. May God bless the people of South Africa.

PEACE IS A DAY-TO-DAY PROBLEM, THE PRODUCT OF A MULTITUDE OF EVENTS AND JUDGMENTS. PEACE IS NOT AN 'IS,' IT IS A 'BECOMING.'

—Haile Selassie,
in an address to the United Nations (1963)

"PEACE AND FRIENDSHIP WITH ALL MANKIND IS OUR WISEST POLICY, AND I WISH WE MAY BE PERMITTED TO PURSUE IT."

—Thomas Jefferson,
in a letter to W. F. Dumas (1786)

OUR PEACE SHALL STAND AS FIRM AS ROCKY MOUNTAINS.

—William Shakespeare, *Henry IV, Part II*

LOCKSLEY HALL

ALFRED, LORD TENNYSON

For I dipt into the future, far as human eye could see,
Saw the Vision of the world, and all the wonder that
would be;

Saw the heavens fill with commerce, argosies of magic
sails,
Pilots of the purple twilight, dropping down with costly
bales;

Heard the heavens fill with shouting, and there rain'd a
ghastly dew
From the nations' airy navies grappling in the central
blue;

Far along the world-wide whisper of the south-wind
rushing warm,
With the standards of the peoples plunging thro' the
thunder-storm;

Till the war-drum throbb'd no longer, and the battle
flags were furl'd
In the Parliament of man, the Federation of the world.

There the common sense of most shall hold a fretful
realm in awe,
And the kindly earth shall slumber, lapt in universal law.

EXCERPT FROM
1964 GREAT SOCIETY SPEECH
AT THE UNIVERSITY OF MICHIGAN

LYNDON B. JOHNSON

The purpose of protecting the life of our nation and preserving the liberty of our citizens is to pursue the happiness of our people. Our success in that pursuit is the test of our success as a nation.

For a century we labored to settle and to subdue a continent. For half a century we called upon unbounded invention and untiring industry to create an order of plenty for all of our people.

The challenge of the next half century is whether we have the wisdom to use that wealth to enrich and elevate our national life, and to advance the quality of our American civilization.

Your imagination and your initiative, and your indignation, will determine whether we build a society where progress is the servant of our needs, or a society where old values and new visions are buried under unbridled growth. For in your time we have the opportunity to move not only toward the rich society and the powerful society, but upward to the Great Society.

The Great Society rests on abundance and liberty for all. It demands an end to poverty and racial injustice, to which we are totally committed in our time. But that is just the beginning.

The Great Society is a place where every child can find knowledge to enrich his mind and to enlarge his talents. It is a place where leisure is a welcome chance to build and reflect, not a feared cause of boredom and restlessness. It is a place where the city of man serves not only the needs of the body and the demands of commerce but the desire for beauty and the hunger for community.

It is a place where man can renew contact with nature. It is a place which honors creation for its own sake and for what it adds to the understanding of the race. It is a place where men are more concerned with the quality of their goals than the quantity of their goods.

But most of all, the Great Society is not a safe harbor, a resting place, a final objective, a finished work. It is a challenge constantly renewed, beckoning us toward a destiny where the meaning of our lives matches the marvelous products of our labor.

FIRE AND ICE
ROBERT FROST

Some say the world will end in fire,

Some say in ice.

From what I've tasted of desire

I hold with those who favor fire.

But if it had to perish twice,

I think I know enough of hate

To say that for destruction ice

Is also great

And would suffice.

"PEACE IS NOT
MERELY A DISTANT
GOAL THAT WE
SEEK, BUT A
MEANS BY WHICH
WE ARRIVE AT
THAT GOAL."

—Martin Luther King Jr.

"IF YOU WANT PEACE, WORK FOR JUSTICE."

—Pope Paul VI

I MANY TIMES THOUGHT PEACE HAD COME

EMILY DICKINSON

I many times thought Peace had come
When Peace was far away—
As Wrecked Men—deem they sight the Land—
At Centre of the Sea—

And struggle slacker—but to prove
As hopelessly as I—
How many the fictitious Shores—
Before the Harbor be—

1948 "THE STRUGGLE FOR HUMAN RIGHTS" SPEECH

IN THE SORBONNE, PARIS

ELEANOR ROOSEVELT

It is my belief, and I am sure it is also yours, that the struggle for democracy and freedom is a critical struggle, for their preservation is essential to the great objective of the United Nations to maintain international peace and security.

Among free men the end cannot justify the means. We know the patterns of totalitarianism—the single political party, the control of schools, press, radio, the arts, the sciences, and the church to support autocratic authority; these are the age-old patterns against which men have struggled for three thousand years. These are the signs of reaction, retreat, and retrogression.

The United Nations must hold fast to the heritage of freedom won by the struggle of its peoples; it must help us to pass it on to generations to come.

The development of the ideal of freedom and its translation into the everyday life of the people in great areas of the Earth is the product of the efforts of many peoples. It is the fruit of a long tradition of vigorous thinking and courageous action. No one race and no one people can claim to have done all the work to achieve greater dignity for human beings and greater freedom to develop human personality. In each generation and in each country there must be a continuation of the struggle and new steps forward must be taken since this is preeminently a field in which to stand still is to retreat.

The field of human rights in not one in which compromise on fundamental principles are possible. The work of the Commission on Human Rights is illustrative. The Declaration of Human Rights provides: "Everyone has the right to leave any country, including his own." The Soviet Representative said he would agree to this right if a single phrase was added to it—"in accordance with the procedure laid down in the laws of that country." It is obvious that to accept this would be not only to compromise but to nullify the right stated. This case forcefully illustrates the importance of the proposition that we must ever be alert not to compromise fundamental human rights merely for the sake of reaching unanimity and thus lose them.

As I see it, it is not going to be easy to attain unanimity with respect to our different concepts of government and human rights. The struggle is bound to be difficult and one in which we must be firm but patient. If we adhere faithfully to our principles I think it is possible for us to maintain freedom and to do so peacefully and without recourse to force.

GETTYSBURG ADDRESS

ABRAHAM LINCOLN

Four score and seven years ago our fathers brought forth on this continent, a new nation, conceived in Liberty, and dedicated to the proposition that all men are created equal.

Now we are engaged in a great civil war, testing whether that nation, or any nation so conceived and so dedicated, can long endure. We are met on a great battle-field of that war. We have come to dedicate a portion of that field, as a final resting place for those who here gave their lives that, that nation might live. It is altogether fitting and proper that we should do this.

But, in a larger sense, we cannot dedicate—we cannot consecrate—we cannot hallow—this ground. The brave men, living and dead, who struggled here, have consecrated it, far above our poor power to add or detract. The world will little note, nor long remember what we say here, but it can never forget what they did here. It is for us the living, rather, to be dedicated here to the unfinished work which they who fought here have thus far so nobly advanced. It is rather for us to be here dedicated to the great task remaining before us—that from these honored dead we take increased devotion to that cause for which they gave the last full measure of devotion—that we here highly resolve that these dead shall not have died in vain—that this nation, under God, shall have a new birth of freedom—and that government of the people, by the people, for the people, shall not perish from the earth.

"THE MORE WE
SWEAT IN PEACE,
THE LESS WE
BLEED IN WAR."

—Vijaya Lakshmi Pandit

ABOUT CIDER MILL PRESS BOOK PUBLISHERS

Good ideas ripen with time. From seed to harvest, Cider Mill Press brings fine reading, information, and entertainment together between the covers of its creatively crafted books. Our Cider Mill bears fruit twice a year, publishing a new crop of titles each spring and fall.

"Where Good Books Are Ready for Press"

Visit us online at
cidermillpress.com

or write to us at
PO Box 454
12 Spring St.
Kennebunkport, Maine 04046